I0800702

STONE AGE SCIENCE

BUILDINGS AND STRUCTURES

Inventions that changed the world—and the science behind them

WRITTEN BY FELICIA LAW & GERRY BAILEY
ILLUSTRATED BY MIKE PHILLIPS

Crabtree Publishing Company
www.crabtreebooks.com
1-800-387-7650

Published in Canada
616 Welland Ave.
St. Catharines, ON
L2M 5V6

Published in the United States
PMB 59051, 350 Fifth Ave.
59th Floor,
New York, NY 10118

Published in **2016 by CRABTREE PUBLISHING COMPANY.**
All rights reserved. No part of this publication may be reproduced, stored in a retrieval system, or transmitted in any form or by any means, electronic, mechanical, photocopy, recording or otherwise, without the prior written permission of the copyright owner.

Authors: Felicia Law and Gerry Bailey
Illustrators: Mike Phillips, Henu Studio
Editors: Shirley Duke, Kathy Middleton
Proofreader: Wendy Scavuzzo
Production coordinator and Prepress technician: Tammy McGarr
Print coordinator: Margaret Amy Salter

Copyright © 2015 BrambleKids Ltd.

Photo credits:
Cover and p1- David M. Schrader
p6 top- WitR; bottom- bibiphoto
p10 top- Monkey Business Images; middle- Stanzi; bottom- Oleg Mikhaylov p14 top- Ian Law; bottom- pinngr
p17 top- Martin Fowler; middle- Bob Mawby; bottom- Paul J Martin
p18 top-Adam Gregor; middle- holbox; bottom- ollirg
p21 top- User Serinde Wikipedia; middle- Raunaq Gupta Wikipedia; bottom-1954 portrait by Al Ravenna, New York World - Telegram and the Sun staff photographer
p23 top- gosphotodesign; bottom- Flashon Studio
p25 top- Sirano100; bottom- Fedor Selivanov p28 top- Bruce Amos; middle- Stephen Finn; bottom- S-F

Printed in the USA/082015/SN20150529

Library and Archives Canada Cataloguing in Publication

Law, Felicia, author
Stone age science : Buildings and structures / Felicia Law, Gerry Bailey; Mike Phillips, illustrator.

(Stone Age science)
Includes index.
Issued in print and electronic formats.
ISBN 978-0-7787-1887-1 (bound).--ISBN 978-0-7787-1911-3 (paperback).--
ISBN 978-1-4271-1676-5 (pdf).--ISBN 978-1-4271-1672-7 (html)

1. Buildings--Juvenile literature. 2. Structural engineering--Juvenile literature. I. Bailey, Gerry, 1945-, author II. Phillips, Mike, 1961-, illustrator III. Title.

TA634.L38 2015 j624.1 C2015-903154-0
C2015-903155-9

Library of Congress Cataloging-in-Publication Data

Law, Felicia, author.
Stone age science : buildings and structures / Felicia Law & Gerry Bailey ; illustrated by Mike Phillips.
pages cm. -- (Stone age science)
Includes index.
ISBN 978-0-7787-1887-1 (reinforced library binding) --
ISBN 978-0-7787-1911-3 (pbk.) --
ISBN 978-1-4271-1676-5 (electronic pdf) --
ISBN 978-1-4271-1672-7 (electronic html)
1. Structural engineering--Juvenile literature. I. Bailey, Gerry, 1945- author. II. Phillips, Mike, 1961- illustrator. III. Title.

TA634.L39 2016
624.1--dc23

2015019248

CONTENTS

MEET LEO

Meet Leo, the brightest kid on the block.

So that's Leo!

Bright as in IQ off the scale, inventive as in Leonardo da Vinci inventive, and way, way ahead of his time...

Block as in Stone Age block. Stone Age as in 30,000 years ago.

Then there's Pallas—Leo's pet.

Pallas is wild. His ancestors have been around for millions of years. You won't see many Pallas cats around today, unless you happen to be visiting the icy, cold wasteland of Arctic Siberia in northern Russia.

And there's a cast of other characters who are all inventors—sort of!

THE ROAD

"Roads are for getting from A to B as quickly as possible," says Leo. "So, we're going to build a road."

Pallas is confused. He often goes from A to B as quickly as possible when he's chasing a mouse, and he has never used a road in his life. He's also suspicious. Whenever Leo talks about building things, it usually means hard work.

"The paths through the woods are full of holes," says Leo. "They sink in the middle. When it rains, all the water collects inside them in large puddles. It doesn't drain off.

And hills and valleys get in the way. The new road will go straight. Nothing will get in its way!"

And just as Pallas thought, Leo has a plan that means hard work for him.

PALLAS SUGGESTS...

- *They could carry a mop and bucket with them to keep the paths free of water.*
- *They could walk on stilts to keep their feet dry. Or, if the road was built higher than the land on either side of it, then the water might run off anyway.*

The ancient Romans always built roads in straight lines. Their roads would pass right over hills instead of going around them. In fact, the Romans constructed over 50,000 miles (80,000 km) of roads that stretched across their huge empire.

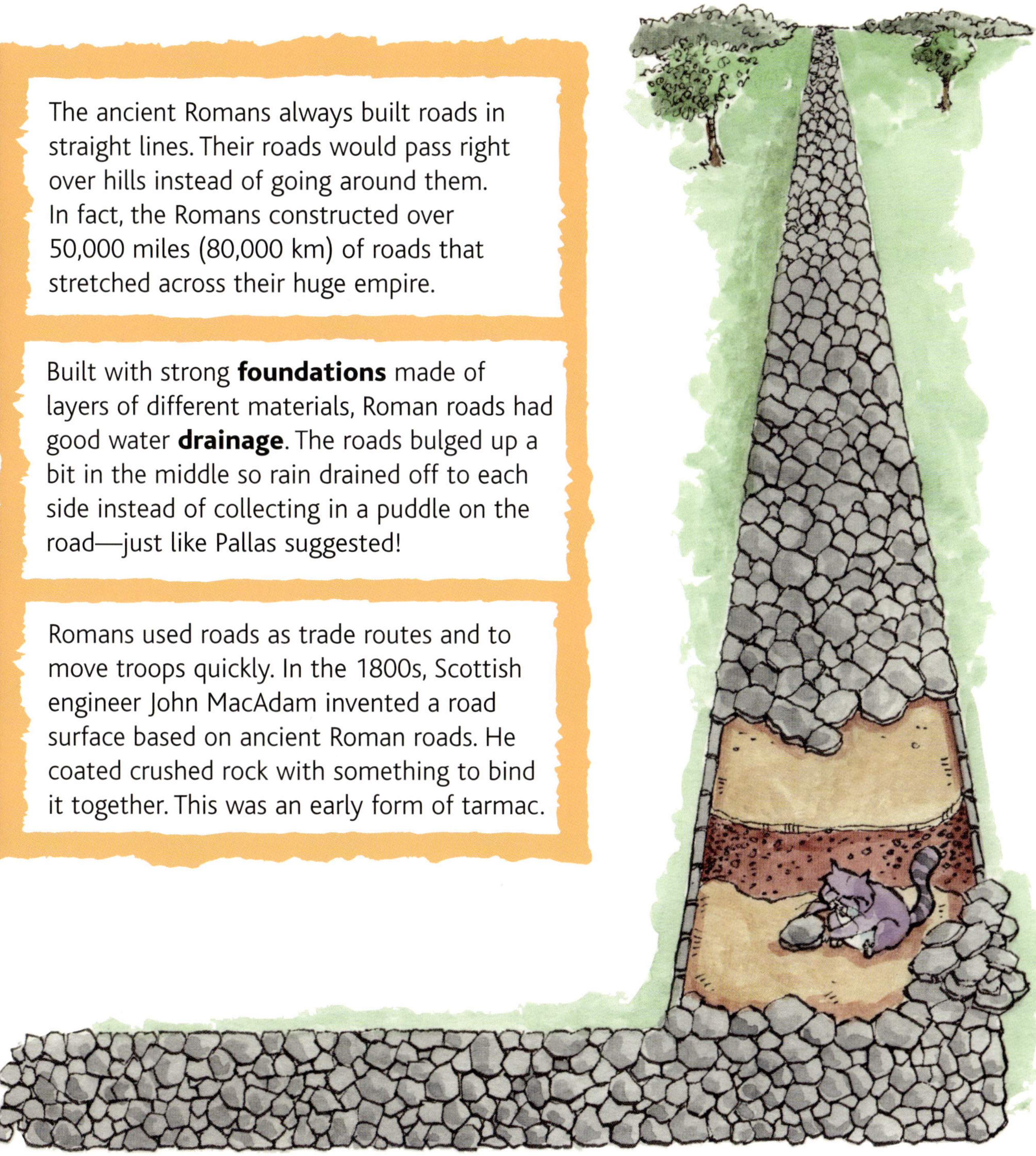

Built with strong **foundations** made of layers of different materials, Roman roads had good water **drainage**. The roads bulged up a bit in the middle so rain drained off to each side instead of collecting in a puddle on the road—just like Pallas suggested!

Romans used roads as trade routes and to move troops quickly. In the 1800s, Scottish engineer John MacAdam invented a road surface based on ancient Roman roads. He coated crushed rock with something to bind it together. This was an early form of tarmac.

FOUNDATIONS AND SURFACES

The roads the Romans made were built on top of foundations—the layers of the road underneath the surface. First there was a layer of sand and crushed stones, then a layer of concrete, then a layer of gravel and rough sand. Finally a layer of flat stones, called paving stones, at least 9.8 inches (25 cm) deep was laid on top.

If water pools on the road, it wears the rock away creating holes that need repair. Good drainage helped Roman roads avoid needing repair.

A road going in a straight line was built with **slopes** going downward from the road's **crown**, or center, to each side of the road. **Gravity** pulls the water downward off the road. For curved roads, such as on a bend, the road was built with a slope across the entire road from the long side down to the short side.

Modern roads are flattened and paved by heavy, slow-moving machines.

Modern roads have a surface made of asphalt, which is a mixture of sand and tar. Tar is a thick, black liquid made from oil products. The asphalt is mixed with crushed stones. This mixture is laid over the layers of material that form the foundations, then it hardens.

BUILD A ROMAN ROAD

You will need

- *a long cardboard box*
- *thick and thin posterboard*
- *double-sided tape*
- *strong glue*
- *flat stones (or slate), pebbles, small rocks, gravel, sand*
- *paint*
- *a paintbrush*

1. ***Glue the long cardboard box to the base of a large piece of thick posterboard.***

2. ***Curve a piece of thin posterboard to make an arch. Tape it to the top of the box. Stick a semicircle of posterboard onto the front of the bulge to cover the hole left by the arch.***

3. ***Draw a square on the front of the model, and glue on the stones. Start with pebbles at the bottom, then small rocks, then gravel, then sand. Glue the flat stones for paving on the top of the cardboard box.***

4. ***Paint the rest of the front part brown for earth. On top, paint both sides of the road green for grass.***

5. ***Paint a hillside scene on the back panel. Show the road disappearing into the distance. Make a Roman figure to stand on your road.***

THE RAMP

"That pyramid of stones has to be moved," says Leo. "It's in the way."

Pallas wants to know what it's in the way of. It doesn't look like a pile of stones that is causing anyone any trouble.

But Leo is determined.
"There's a new road coming through this way," he says, "and that pyramid is in the way. We have to move it from over there to over here."

He tells everyone to help with the heavy work by forming a chain. As each stone is removed from the pile, it can be passed from one to the other until it's out of the way.

Taking the stones down is easy work. Lifting them up to make a new pyramid is not!

PALLAS SUGGESTS...

- *Maybe if Mammoth could be used like a bulldozer, she could just knock the pile down.*

- *Another idea—why not roll the stones down from the top? Things roll down a slope very quickly once they get started.*

An earth ramp is a solid surface with a slope, made of soil or rocks and soil tightly packed together. Since it is solid, it is very sturdy and can support very heavy weights.

Heavy objects can be rolled down or rolled up a ramp. Earth ramps were used to help build many ancient buildings and monuments. The ancient Egyptians built earth ramps to drag up huge blocks of stone when they built the pyramids.

Early engineers also used smaller earth ramps to haul up **lintels**, or top stones, and ease them into place across the top of two stones. This is how the Stonehenge monument in Britain was built many thousands of years ago.

RAISING LOADS

A sloping surface that links two places at different levels is called a ramp. It is also known as an **inclined plane**.

If a heavy barrel needs to be lifted straight up onto a high rack, it could only be lifted by a strong person. This would be hard work. The muscle power needed would have to match the barrel's weight, called its **load**.

Ramps are used to get wheelchairs into and out of vehicles.

Instead, the barrel could be rolled up a ramp. Using a ramp is easier because the **force** needed to push is less than the force needed for lifting up. The barrel does need to be pushed a longer distance than lifting straight up would require. But increasing the distance the barrel moves decreases the effort needed to move it.

The hens use a ramp to reach their henhouse.

Skateboarders sometimes use a ramp to give them more speed. The steeper the ramp, the faster gravity pulls them downward. However, the ramp also allows a skateboarder to control his or her speed because gravity is reduced by the upward push of the ramp itself.

A skateboarder uses ramps to do tricks as well as to increase speed.

MEASURE THE FORCE

You will need

- *a flat board, about 20–28 inches (50–70 cm) long*
- *a pencil*
- *a ruler*
- *a drinking straw*
- *a rubber band*
- *a thin skewer or straightened wire coat hanger*
- *a toothpick*
- *a pushpin*
- *a small toy truck filled with sand or gravel*
- *string*

1. ***Mark a scale in inches or centimeters on the flat board using a pencil and ruler.***

2. ***Cut a length of drinking straw about 1.2 inches (3 cm) long. Push the rubber band through it, using the skewer or wire hanger.***

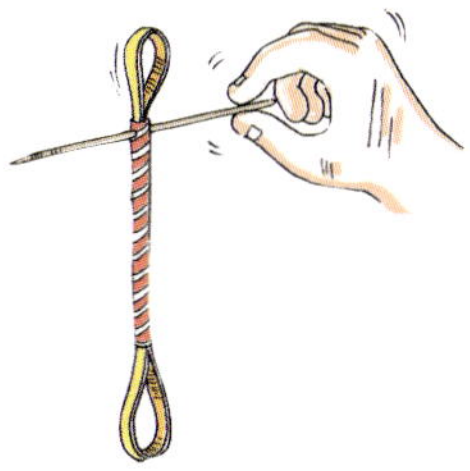

3. ***Make a pinhole through the straw, then push the toothpick through the hole so it holds one end of the rubber band.***

4. ***Tie a string to the front of the truck, then hook this on to the toothpick. Fasten the other end of the rubber band to the board with the pushpin.***

WHAT HAPPENS?

If you stand the board straight up, gravity pulls the truck downward so it stretches to the highest number on your scale. As you lower the top end of the board, it becomes a ramp. The rubber band gradually pulls the truck up more easily as the ramp is made less steep. The numbers on your scale show how much the force required to move the truck decreases.

THE BRIDGE

It has been raining all day. The stream is swollen and is flooding its banks. When Leo tries to cross, he must wade through up to his waist.

"What we need," he says, "is a way of crossing that keeps us dry."

Pallas agrees. He has the usual cat thing about water. Like most cats, he hates it.

Mammoth isn't that fond of water, either. Her long, hairy coat gets soggy and heavy, and weighs her down. "You could get yourself a boat," Mammoth suggests. "Something that keeps you dry, gets you over the stream, and isn't me."

PALLAS SUGGESTS...

- *If Leo doesn't like getting his feet wet, he should wear waterproof boots.*
- *Another way to stay well above the water level would be to cross the stream on stilts. He just needs to be above the water level.*

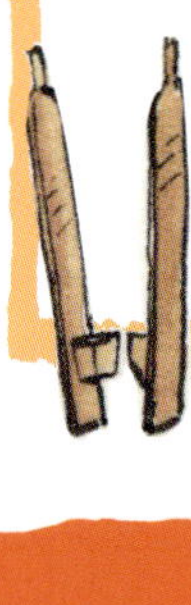

The very first bridges may have been made from tree trunks. People built clapper bridges thousands of years ago. They were among the first bridges ever to have been built.

Most clapper bridges are made by balancing flat stones on top of each other to make a **pier**, or supporting post. Other larger stones are then placed across the piers as stepping stones.

The Tarr Steps cross the River Barle in Exmoor National Park in England. This bridge is about 3,000 years old!

A 17-step clapper bridge

An arched clapper bridge

STRESS AND STRAIN

Stress is a force or pressure. Stress can make an object change its shape. It can compress, or squash, something, or it can stretch and expand it. When scientists and engineers talk about calculating stress, they are talking about how to measure the pressure being put on something.

Stress and **strain** go together. Strain measures how much the shape of an object changes under stress, or how much it bends. The greater the stress, the greater the strain, and the more an object will bend. If the stress on an object is too great, the object may even break.

A bridge must be built so it is strong enough to resist the stress of traffic and people traveling over it. The cables that attach the bridge to the upright piers along its length are usually made of steel. These help spread the load from the bridge back to the piers and into the ground. This kind of bridge is called a **suspension bridge**.

Tower Bridge in London is a suspension bridge. Two side-by-side walkways across the top help ease the pull from the suspension cables.

This rope bridge bends easily with the stress caused by people walking over it.

A modern suspension bridge

THREE BRIDGES

You will need

- ***newspaper***
- ***glue***
- ***thick cardboard***
- ***paint***
- ***several small stones and flat pebbles***
- ***thin posterboard***
- ***wooden toothpicks or skewers***
- ***string***
- ***scissors***

For the landscape, scrunch up newspaper to make hills, and glue it to the thick cardboard (shown at left). Between the hills, paste down newspaper scraps to make a smooth surface for the river. Paint the hills and the river.

BEAM BRIDGE

Fold a narrow strip of thin posterboard lengthwise. Cut small rectangles of posterboard and glue them to the bridge to make paving slabs. Glue the bridge to the sides of the hill.

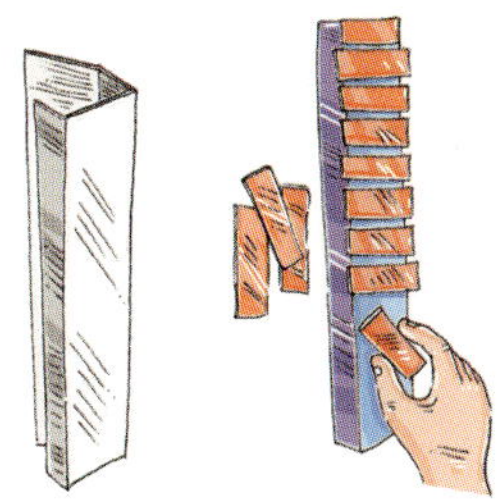

beam bridge

suspension bridge

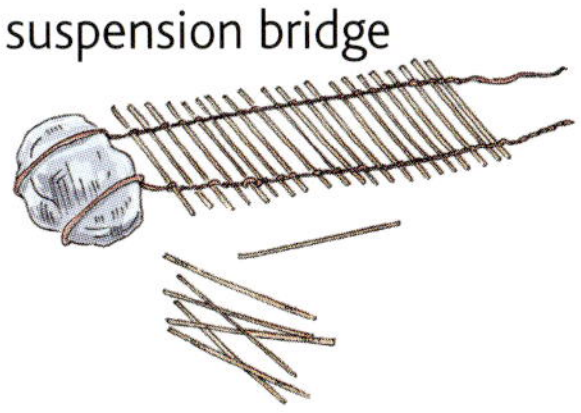

SUSPENSION BRIDGE

Break toothpicks into equal lengths, about 2 inches (5 cm). Tie a string around one end of each toothpick, making a row. Do the same on the other side so it looks like train tracks. Tie the ends of the strings around stones.

CLAPPER BRIDGE

To make a clapper bridge, place small stones on the river for the piers and flat pebbles on top of them for the path across.

clapper bridge

THE ARCH

Whenever Leo and Pallas cross the wooden bridge, it wobbles. It shakes and sways. Pallas doesn't like wobbling and swaying.

(It also sags, but Pallas knows he's a heavy cat who makes bridges sag, so he doesn't mention this.)

"Okay," says Leo. "You're just being a scaredy-cat, but I'll fix it." And he looks for a stronger board.

But when Mammoth wants to cross the bridge, too, Leo gets worried. The weight of Mammoth will certainly make the bridge bend even more—it might even snap!

PALLAS SUGGESTS...

- *Leo could fill the ravine with rocks and rubble until the wall of pebbles reaches the top and helps to support the plank.*
- *Pallas says a mammoth-sized stool ought to hold Mammoth's weight, so why not build the bridge with support like a giant stool?*

Bridges need to be as strong as possible to support the weight of people, cars, and heavy trucks that travel across it. They must also stand up to the force of winds—and sometimes even earthquakes!—that push and pull on them.

Over 4,000 years ago, engineers discovered that the shape of an **arch** could be used to add strength to the design of a bridge.

When an arch is built, the stone blocks are cut into wedge shapes that narrow at one end. When they are wedged against each other to form the arch, they push against each other, giving strength to the whole arch.

The very last wedge-shaped stone, called the **keystone**, fits into the middle of the arch. It is the keystone that locks the arch together.

FORCES AND LOADS

An arch is a curved structure. It is used as a strong supporting link to **span**, or cross, the distance between two pillars or piers. Arches are often used in bridge design. They are able to support the weight of the bridge itself, as well as the weight of whatever is traveling over it, called the load.

The keystone can be seen clearly in the center above this arched gate.

An arch **redistributes**, or spreads out, the load by pushing it outward and spreading it down the supports at the sides of the bridge. Instead of the heavy load pushing down on the top of the bridge, it pushes outward to the supports.

Arches form an important part of this Roman aqueduct in Segovia, Spain. An aqueduct is a canal built on a bridge that carries water from one place to another.

The force of the load is spread out across the whole bridge. This means that an arched bridge can carry heavier loads than a normal, flat-topped bridge, as long as there are strong supports on both sides of the arch.

FITTING THE KEYSTONE

You will need

- *string*
- *a cardboard tube about 20 inches (50 cm) long and about 1.2 inches (3 cm) in diameter (or roll one from a sheet of thin posterboard)*
- *a board or shallow box about 20 x 12 inches (50 x 30 cm)*
- *paint*
- *wrapping paper*
- *10–12 plastic drinking cups*
- *glue*
- *tape*

1. ***Pull the string through the cardboard tube and tape the ends to the bottom of the board. If you like, paint the board and tube, or decorate it with wrapping paper.***

2. ***Glue or tape two cups to the outside bottom edges of the board. Make sure the bottoms of the cups face each other***

3. ***Add the other cups to the board in a semicircle, but don't attach them. Then stand it up. The cups will stay in position, just like the arch of a bridge.***

4. ***Try filling the middle cup—your keystone—with stones or rice. The arch should easily withstand the weight.***

OOPS!!
Remove the keystone cup and see what happens to your bridge!

FRANK LLOYD WRIGHT

A MAMMOTH INVENTOR!

As a young boy, Frank Lloyd Wright spent a lot of time playing with blocks. He discovered the shapes could be put together in various combinations to form **three-dimensional (3-D)** shapes. Many of his buildings are built in simple shapes such as triangles, cubes, or pentagons.

Frank left high school shortly before graduation, and quickly found work with an **architect**. He joined other architects and learned all he could from them. In 1893, he left to open his own office as an architect.

Frank's designs were heavily influenced by nature, the shape of the land, and the colors and patterns of plants. He also tried to build with natural, instead of human-made, materials.

Of the over 1,000 buildings Frank Lloyd Wright designed, 532 were actually built. He is considered the greatest American architect of all time. Some of his buildings are so special, they have been nominated to be **World Heritage sites**.

ARCHITECTURE

Architects make detailed drawings and plans of their new buildings. They may also build a model to show how the building will fit into the landscape. Wright's model of Fallingwater (shown below) is in the Carnegie Science Center in Pittsburgh.

Fallingwater is one of Frank Lloyd Wright's most well-known buildings. It reflects the natural woods and river that surround it.

BUILDING WALLS

Leo has had enough! His latest idea is a garden. But each time he plants vegetables, they mysteriously disappear. The carrots, cabbages, potatoes, and turnips grow fat and ripe, then they're gone.

Pallas says he can't help. He's not the thief. He doesn't like vegetables very much. In fact, he's never eaten one in his life.

"It probably isn't a cat," he tells Leo.

But Leo is not so sure. All the animals seem to be taking a lot of interest in his vegetables.

"They may just be interested in gardening," suggests Pallas.

But Leo decides to take action. He needs to protect his vegetables in some way, and that's not going to be easy.

PALLAS SUGGESTS...

The easiest way is to tell people to stay out of the garden—and that means a sign.

- *Perhaps Pallas could stand guard over the vegetables and catch the thief—he'd be happy to help as long as the thief were a mouse.*

STRESS

A wall is a structure. Walls are used to enclose an area or as support structures in a building. They are strong enough to resist outside forces such as wind and rain. They also support the roof—a heavy load that presses down on the walls.

Modern walls are made of strong materials that can resist stress from the forces that push against them. These materials include bricks and mortar. Mortar is made of a mixture of sand, cement, and water. The hardened mixture adds strength to a brick structure.

In low buildings that have no more than four stories, or floors, the load is transmitted, or moved, through the walls to the foundations. Strong foundations support the weight of the walls and roof, and keep the building from falling down.

Bricks held together with mortar are the basic materials of a wall.

Centuries ago, the Great Wall of China was built with bricks to keep enemies out.

HOMES ON STILTS

Leo plans to build a home that is high off the ground on strong wooden poles called **stilts**. If the river floods its banks, he won't get wet. Plus, he will feel safer at night when hungry saber-tooth cats are prowling outside.

But first he has to make sure the stilts in the ground are standing perfectly upright. That's the only way they will be able to stand up to the load of the floor and walls above.

"It's a balancing act," Leo says.

Pallas agrees. He tries to help, but getting the poles to stay straight isn't easy.

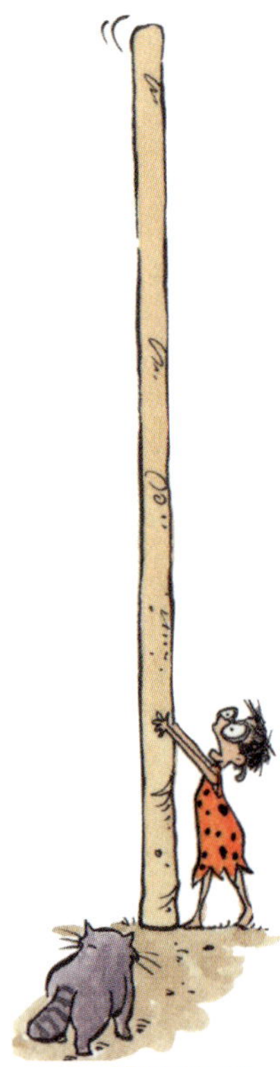

After a long struggle, they get four poles upright in the ground. These will be the four corners of Leo's new house. He hopes they are all even or it might become known as the leaning stilt-house of Leo.

BALANCE POINT

In rainy or wet places, or where there may be dangerous animals, homes are sometimes built on stilts. These kinds of houses can still be seen in parts of Asia today. The stilts are strong wooden poles. The stilts must be placed underneath the structure in a way that evenly balances the forces pushing and pulling on it.

Houses built on stilts have a balance point in the center of the structure.

This means that the force pushing upward from the ground through the poles must equal the force of gravity pulling down on the structure. Most important, the forces have to be equal at all four corners. If one corner pole is removed, the house can collapse.

Any structure that is balanced in this way must have a **balance point**. This is the one place where all the pulling and pushing forces are equal. All objects—even people—have a balance point. This is usually the center point of the object or the middle of the person.

The balance point in the middle of the Leaning Tower of Pisa is still above the tower's base. This keeps it from falling over.

THE SKYSCRAPER

"It would be fun to live up there," says Leo, gazing up at the tall pile of boulders. "We could build a home on the top with fantastic views."

Pallas is fine with the idea of fantastic views, but the whole thing looks a bit shaky to him.

"We could all live there," says Leo, "each home stacked on top of the others. Building upward won't take up as much land as building outward. We can share the stairway. We'll even share heat from a furnace in the basement and fresh air blowing from fans. Now I just have to figure out how to build it."

Pallas is fine with the idea of sharing a new home. He's fine with the idea of sharing most things. He just wonders if anyone will want to share the hard work of building it.

PALLAS SUGGESTS...

- *If Leo wants to live high up, he'll need some way of climbing there. He should have at least one ladder, if not more.*

- *A high building needs a strong frame. Leo will need lots of tall poles in the ground to form this frame.*

A **skyscraper** is a tall building with many stories. Most skyscrapers are built on a **frame** made of steel **girders**, or beams.

The first skyscraper built this way was the 138-foot- (42 m) high Home Insurance Building in Chicago. Designed by American architect William Jenney, it was completed in 1885. Today, the tallest building in the world is in Dubai in the United Arab Emirates, reaching 2,723 feet (830 meters).

Skyscrapers have two main sections that help support the building: the part below ground, called the **foundation**, and the part above ground, called the **superstructure**.

When skyscrapers are over 40 stories high, it is important for the structure's safety that the frame can bear the force of high winds.

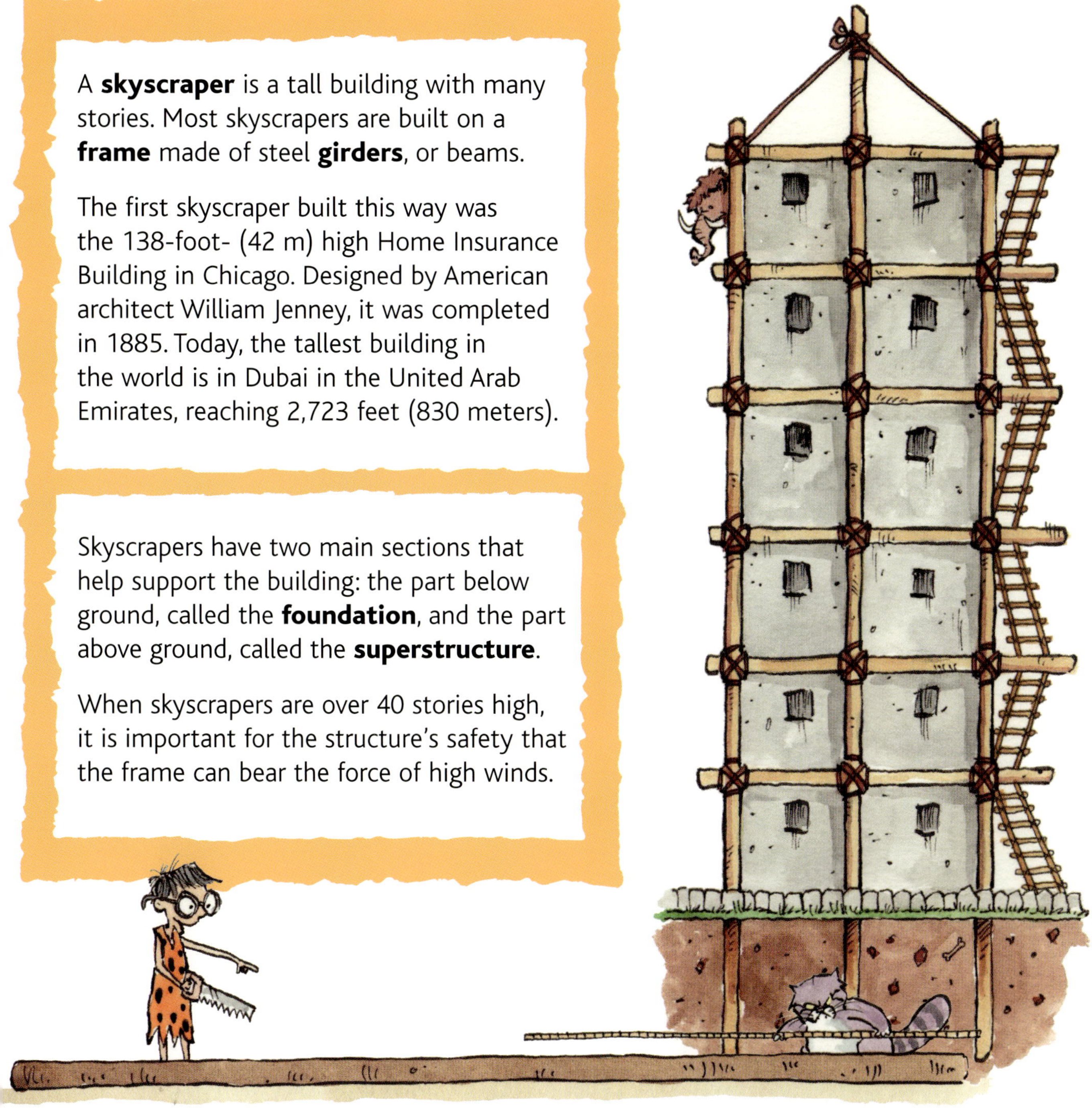

FRAMEWORK

Engineers and architects who construct, or build, skyscrapers talk about the load of a building. A load is a weight. It is the weight that a force pushes against.

The frame of this building is made of steel and concrete slabs that lock together.

In addition to a foundation, a skyscraper must be built with a steel or **concrete** frame inside. This helps support the load of the building, just like your skeleton supports you. In a skyscraper, the walls hang on the frame. This means the load does not move through the walls to the foundation. Instead, the loads of the walls, roof, and floors are carried by the frame.

Steel girders form the framework of a skyscraper.

Steel beams, called girders, form a frame around which the walls of the building are fitted. Concrete, a mixture of cement, water, and crushed stones, is used to hold the materials together.

Piles made of concrete and steel are sunk into holes in the ground to anchor, or securely hold, the building.

Burj Khalifa, in Dubai, is the tallest skyscraper in the world.

MAKE A SKYSCRAPER

You will need

- *thick posterboard*
- *a pencil*
- *a ruler*
- *yogurt cups*
- *plastic bottles*
- *straws*
- *paint and a paintbrush*
- *scissors*
- *glue*

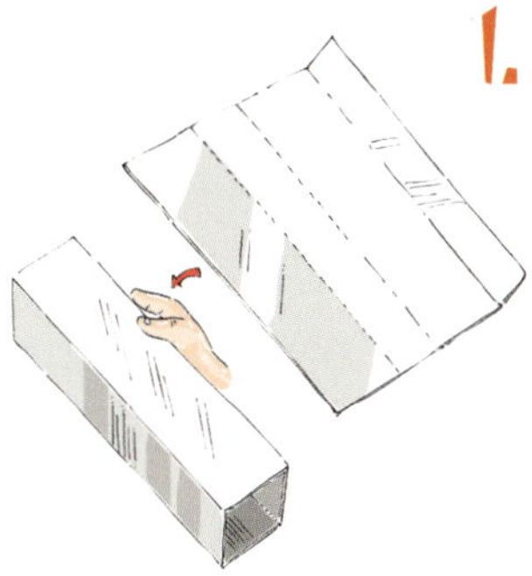

1. *Fold the thick posterboard lengthwise into four equal sections. Tape it into a rectangular column.*

2. *Mark off the stories. Evenly space them going up the column. Draw in some floor features, such as doors, stairs, an elevator, and entrances.*

3. *Cut out a rectangular piece of posterboard, then cut a square in the center with flaps where the column will fit through. Use this as a template for making as many floors as you like. Now decorate each floor in a different color.*

4. *For support, insert small posts made from posterboard at the four corners of each floor. You can also stick paper walls onto two sides of the building.*

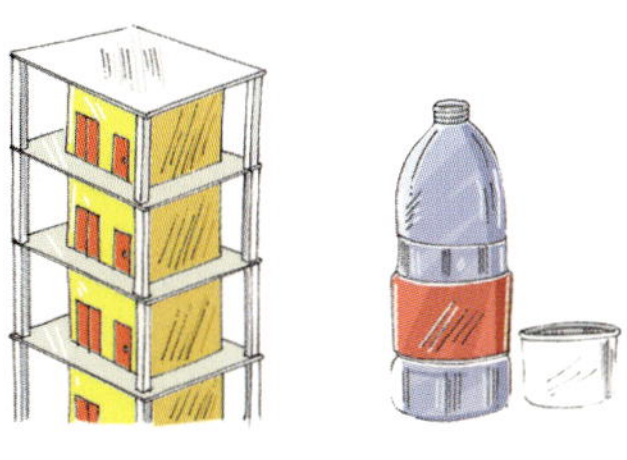

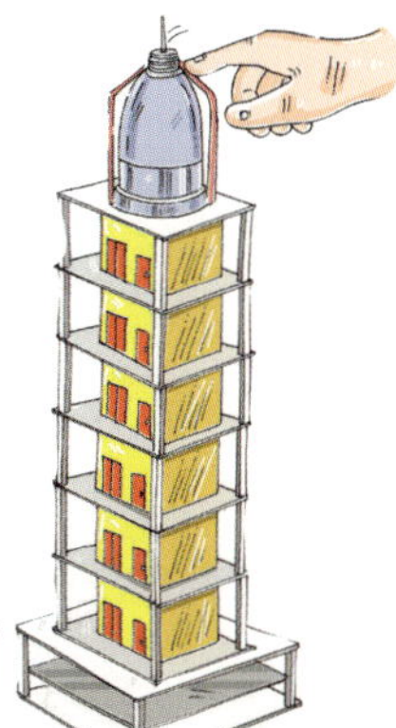

5. *Construct a roof spire from bottles, cups, and straws. Spray it with silver paint and glue it to the top of your skyscraper.*

BALANCE THE POTATO

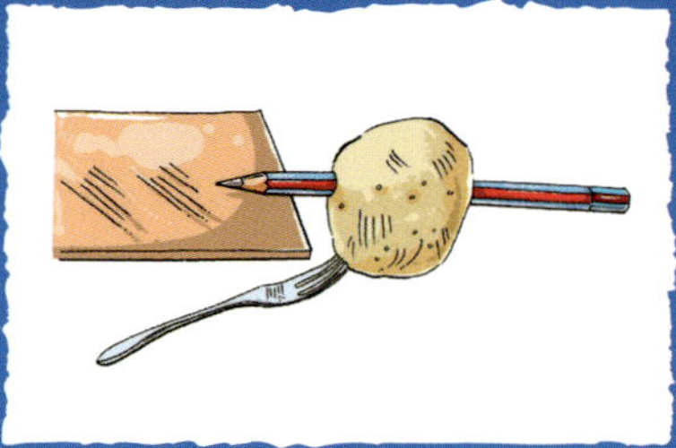

You will need:

- a wooden pencil with a sharp point
- a small potato • a fork • a table

1. Press the sharp point of the pencil right through the potato until it sticks 0.6 of an inch (1.5 cm) out the other side. Push the fork in at an angle.
2. Place the pencil tip on the edge of the table until the potato balances.
3. If it does not balance, change the angle of the fork or move the pencil. There is just ONE point where the whole thing will balance, so continue to experiment until you find it.

BALANCE THE CLOWN

You will need

- a large index card
- a pencil with eraser
- scissors
- markers
- paper clips
- string

1. To make a symmetrical clown, fold an index card in half and draw half of the clown. The fold line in the middle of the card is the middle of the clown.
2. Cut out the clown through both layers, then unfold the paper. Decorate. Attach a paper clip to each arm for weight.
3. Try balancing the clown on the eraser of a pencil. Then try balancing the clown with just one paper clip on one arm to see if there is a different effect. Can you figure out the reason for the different results?
4. To balance your clown on a tightrope, tie a string between two chairs and pull it tight. Cut a notch in the clown's hat, and set the notch on the string.

GLOSSARY

Note: Some boldfaced words are defined where they appear in the book.

arch A bent or curved shape that creates strong support in the center that can hold up a bridge

architect A person who designs buildings

balance point The place in a person or object where all forces are balanced equally, keeping the object or person from falling over

concrete A mixture of sand, cement, and water that dries to a strong solid and is useful in building

drainage The action of drawing away or flowing off of water

earth ramp A slope made of packed soil, or earth, that can be used for more easily raising or lowering objects

force A push or a pull action that affects objects

foundation The part of a building, usually underground, which supports a building

frame A structure of beams inside a building that gives support and shape to the walls

gravity A physical force that attracts one body to another

inclined plane A sloping surface that can be used to reduce the work needed to raise or lower a heavy object; It is also called a ramp.

keystone The wedge-shaped stone that is fitted into the center of a stone arch to hold the other stones in place

pier A strong support used to hold up the framework of a building or bridge

pile A pier that is usually sunk deep into the ground to support a heavy building above

skyscraper A building composed of many stories

slope An upward or downward slant

suspension bridge A bridge that is held in place by hanging supports stretched between two piers

three-dimensional (3-D) Having length, width, and height

World Heritage site A place identified by a United Nations organization that is culturally or physically important

LEARNING MORE

Books

Great Building Designs 1900–Today
by Ian Graham.
Heinemann, 2015

Whose Tools?
by Toni Buzzeo and Jim Datz.
Abrams, 2015

Skyscrapers and Towers
By Shirley Duke.
Rourke, 2016

Websites

Read about different structures around the world.
www.sciencekids.co.nz/pictures/structures.html

Use hands-on activities to explore building and structures.
www.exploratorium.edu/structures/

Answer your building questions and find out more about well-known buildings.
www.pbs.org/wgbh/buildingbig/skyscraper/index.html

INDEX